RASPBERRY PI 5 MADE EASY FOR BEGINNERS

A beginner to pro guide to DIY projects, Hacks, home automation and more.

Garry Morrison

INTRODUCTION
What is Raspberry Pi 5

The Raspberry Pi 5 is the latest generation of the popular Raspberry Pi single-board computer. It was released in October 2023 and is the most powerful and versatile Raspberry Pi to date.

The Raspberry Pi 5 features a 2.4GHz quad-core Arm Cortex-A76 processor, up to 8GB of RAM, and a VideoCore VII GPU. It also has dual 4Kp60 HDMI display output, dual-band 802.11ac Wi-Fi, Bluetooth 5.0, 2×

USB 3.0 ports, 2× USB 2.0 ports, and Gigabit Ethernet with PoE+ support. The Raspberry Pi 5 is available in two models: 4GB and 8GB. The 4GB model costs $60, and the 8GB model costs $80.

The Raspberry Pi 5 is a versatile computer that can be used for a wide variety of tasks, including:

- Learning to code
- Building retro gaming consoles
- Setting up a home media centre
- Creating a DIY smart home
- Running server applications

The Raspberry Pi 5 is a great choice for anyone who is looking for a powerful and affordable single-board computer. It is easy to use and has a large community of users and developers.

WHAT'S NEW?

The Raspberry Pi 5 is a significant upgrade over its predecessor, the Raspberry Pi 4, with several new features and improvements. Here are some of the key highlights:

1. Enhanced Performance: The Raspberry Pi 5 boasts a 2.4GHz quad-core Arm Cortex-A76 processor, delivering up to three times faster performance compared to the Raspberry Pi 4. This enhanced power makes the Raspberry Pi 5 ideal for demanding tasks like 4K video playback, gaming, and running resource-intensive applications.

2. Improved Connectivity: The Raspberry Pi 5 features dual-band 802.11ac Wi-Fi and Bluetooth 5.0, ensuring reliable and high-speed wireless connectivity. It also retains Gigabit Ethernet with PoE+ support, providing a stable wired connection option.

3. Dual 4Kp60 HDMI Output:
The Raspberry Pi 5 offers dual 4Kp60 HDMI display output, enabling you to connect two high-resolution monitors for immersive visuals and enhanced productivity. This feature is particularly useful for digital signage, home theater setups, and dual-screen workstations.

4. Increased RAM Options:
The Raspberry Pi 5 comes in two RAM variants: 4GB and 8GB. This expanded RAM capacity allows for smoother multitasking, handling more demanding applications, and running memory-intensive operating systems.

5. PCIe 2.0 Interface: For the first time, the Raspberry Pi 5 introduces a PCIe 2.0 x1 interface. This expansion slot enables the connection of high-bandwidth peripherals, such as faster storage drives, specialized network adapters, and external GPUs.

6. Enhanced I/O Capabilities: The Raspberry Pi 5 retains the standard 40-Pin GPiO header, providing flexibility for interfacing with electronics, sensors, and actuators. It also includes two four-lane MIPi camera/display transceivers, supporting high-resolution cameras and advanced display technologies.

7. Power Button and Real-Time Clock: The Raspberry Pi 5 incorporates a dedicated power button for convenient on/off control, eliminating the need for power adapters that lack a physical switch. It also features a real-time clock, ensuring that the system maintains accurate timekeePing even when power is disconnected.

Overall, the Raspberry Pi 5 represents a significant leap forward in terms of performance, connectivity, versatility, and expandability. It caters to a wider range of users, from hobbyists and educators to professional developers and embedded systems enthusiasts.

CHAPTER ONE

SETTING UP YOUR RASPBERRY Pi 5

Setting up your Raspberry Pi 5 is a straightforward process that involves preparing the hardware, installing the operating system, and configuring the basic settings. Here's a step-by-step guide to get you started:

Gather the Necessary Hardware:

1. Raspberry Pi 5 Board: The Raspberry Pi 5 single-board computer is the heart of the setup.

2. Power Supply: A 5V/3A power supply unit (PSU) is required to provide sufficient power to the Raspberry Pi 5.

3. MicroSD Card: An 8GB or larger microSD card is recommended to store the operating system and applications.

4. HDMI Cable: An HDMI cable is needed to connect the Raspberry Pi 5 to a monitor or TV for display output.

5. USB Keyboard and Mouse: A USB keyboard and mouse are

essential for interacting with the Raspberry Pi 5.

Install the Raspberry Pi OS:

1. Download Raspberry Pi Imager: Install the Raspberry Pi Imager software on your computer. This tool simplifies the process of installing operating systems on Raspberry Pi devices.

2. Prepare the MicroSD Card: Insert the microSD card into your computer's SD card reader. Use Raspberry Pi Imager to format the microSD card as FAT32.

3. Download Raspberry Pi OS Lite: Choose the Raspberry Pi OS Lite (32-bit) operating system from the Raspberry Pi Imager software.

4. Write Raspberry Pi OS to MicroSD Card: Use Raspberry Pi Imager to write the downloaded Raspberry Pi OS Lite image to the formatted microSD card.

5. Safely Eject the MicroSD Card: Once the writing process is complete, safely eject the microSD card from your computer.

Connect and Power Up the Raspberry Pi 5:

1. Insert the MicroSD Card: Insert the microSD card containing the Raspberry Pi OS Lite image into the microSD card slot on the Raspberry Pi 5 board.

2. Connect the Display: Connect the HDMI cable from the Raspberry Pi 5's HDMI port to the HDMI input of your monitor or TV.

3. Connect the Keyboard and Mouse: Plug the USB keyboard and mouse into the USB ports on the Raspberry Pi 5 board.

4. Connect the Power Supply: Connect the 5V/3A power supply unit to the Raspberry Pi 5's power input jack.

5. Power On: Turn on the power supply to boot up the Raspberry Pi 5.

Configure Basic Settings:

1. Initial Setup Wizard: Follow the on-screen instructions provided by the Raspberry Pi OS Lite initial setup wizard.

2. Set Language and Keyboard Layout: Choose your

preferred language and keyboard layout for input.

3. Connect to Wi-Fi: Select your Wi-Fi network and enter the password to establish an internet connection.

4. Set Username and Password: Create a new username and password for your Raspberry Pi 5 user account.

5. Update Software Packages: Use the terminal or the software update application to ensure the installed software packages are up to date.

6. Explore and Customize:
Once the basic setup is complete, you can explore the Raspberry Pi OS Lite environment and customize it to your liking.

Remember that this is a general overview of the setup process. Specific details may vary depending on the version of Raspberry Pi OS and your personal preferences. Refer to the official Raspberry Pi documentation for the most up-to-date information and detailed instructions.

Installing software on your raspberry Pi 5

Installing software on your Raspberry Pi 5 is a straightforward process, allowing you to expand its capabilities and tailor it to your specific needs. There are two primary methods for installing software on Raspberry Pi OS: using the graphical user interface (GUI) or the command line.

Method 1: Using the Graphical User Interface (GUI)

1. Open the Add/Remove Software Application: Click on

the Raspberry Pi icon in the top left corner of the screen, select "Preferences," and then choose "Add/Remove Software."

2. Search for Software: Use the search bar at the top of the application to find the software you want to install.

3. Select and Install Software: Once you've found the desired software, check the box next to its name and click the "Apply" button. The software will be downloaded and installed on your Raspberry Pi 5.

Method 2: Using the Command Line

1. Open a Terminal Window: Click on the terminal icon in the applications menu or press Ctrl+Alt+T to open a terminal window.

2. Update Package Lists: Before installing software, ensure your package lists are up to date by tyPing the following command and pressing Enter:

sudo apt update

3. Install Software: Use the following command to install the desired software, replacing "software_name" with the actual name of the package:

```
sudo apt install software_name
```

4. Enter Password: When prompted, enter your Raspberry Pi user password and press Enter to proceed with the installation.

You can also use the command line to uninstall software by replacing "install" with "remove" in the above command. For example, to uninstall the "software_name" package, type:

sudo apt remove software_name

These methods allow you to easily install and manage software on your Raspberry Pi 5, enabling you to customize it for your specific needs and projects.

CHAPTER TWO

Using the Raspberry Pi As a Desktop Computer

The Raspberry Pi can be a great alternative to a traditional desktop computer for many tasks, especially for those who are on a budget or who want a more compact and versatile device. While the Raspberry Pi is not as powerful as a high-end desktop computer, it is still capable of running many common applications, such as web browsing, email, word processing, and spreadsheets. It can also be used for more demanding tasks, such as video editing and programming.

Here are some of the advantages of using a Raspberry Pi as a desktop computer:

Cost-effective: The Raspberry Pi is a very affordable computer, with the Raspberry Pi 400 costing as little as $35.

Compact and portable: The Raspberry Pi is very small and lightweight, making it easy to transport.

Versatility: The Raspberry Pi can be used for a wide variety of tasks, including web browsing, email, word processing, spreadsheets, video editing, programming, and more.

Low power consumption: The Raspberry Pi is a very energy-efficient device, making it a good choice for those who are concerned about their environmental impact.

Large community: There is a large and active community of Raspberry Pi users, which means that there is a wealth of online resources available to help you get started and troubleshoot any problems you may encounter.

Here are some of the disadvantages of using a Raspberry Pi as a desktop computer:

Limited processing power: While the Raspberry Pi is capable of running many common applications, it is not as powerful as a high-end desktop computer. This means that it may not be able to handle more demanding tasks, such as gaming or video editing.

Limited storage: The Raspberry Pi tyPically comes with a small amount of storage, which can fill up quickly if you install a lot of software or store a lot of files. You can expand the storage by using an external hard drive or microSD card, but this will add to the cost.

Limited connectivity: The Raspberry Pi tyPically only has a few USB ports and an HDMI port, which can limit your connectivity options. You may need to purchase additional adapters or hubs to connect all of your peripherals.

Overall, the Raspberry Pi is a great option for a desktop computer for many people. It is affordable, versatile, and has a large community of users. However, it is important to be aware of its limitations before you make a purchase.

Here are some tips for using a Raspberry Pi as a desktop computer:

Choose the right operating system: There are several different operating systems available for the Raspberry Pi, each with its own strengths and weaknesses. Some popular options include Raspberry Pi OS, Ubuntu Mate, and LibreELEC.

Install the software you need: There are a wide variety of software applications available for the Raspberry Pi, including web browsers, email clients, word processors, spreadsheets, video editors, and programming languages.

Connect your peripherals: You can connect your Raspberry Pi to a variety of peripherals, such as keyboards, mice, monitors, printers, and external hard drives.

Keep your software up to date: It is important to keep your Raspberry Pi's software up to date to ensure that you have the latest security patches and bug fixes.

Join the community: There is a large and active community of Raspberry Pi users who can help you with any problems you may encounter.

With a little planning and effort, you can use your Raspberry Pi as a powerful and versatile desktop computer.

Browsing the web with raspberry Pi 5

There are several great web browsers available for the

Raspberry Pi 5. Here are some of the most popular options:

Chromium: Chromium is the default web browser on Raspberry Pi OS. It is a fast and lightweight browser that is based on the open-source Chromium project.

Mozilla Firefox: Firefox is another popular web browser that is available for the Raspberry Pi 5. It is a more powerful and feature-rich browser than Chromium, but it also uses more resources.

EPiphany: EPiphany is a lightweight web browser that is

based on the WebKit rendering engine. It is a good option for users who have older Raspberry Pi models or who want a more minimalist browsing experience.

Midori: Midori is another lightweight web browser that is based on the WebKit rendering engine. It is a good option for users who have very limited RAM or who want a browser that is designed for touch input.

Puffin: Puffin is a cloud-based web browser that is designed to provide a fast and secure browsing experience on mobile devices. It is

also available for the Raspberry Pi
5.

The best web browser for you will
depend on your individual needs
and preferences. If you are looking
for a fast and lightweight browser,
Chromium is a good option. If you
need a more powerful and
feature-rich browser, Firefox is a
good choice. If you have an older
Raspberry Pi model or limited
RAM, EPiphany or Midori are
good options. And if you want a
fast and secure browsing
experience, Puffin is a good
choice.

Here are some tips for browsing the web with your Raspberry Pi 5:

Use a lightweight web browser: Lightweight web browsers, such as Chromium and EPiphany, will use less RAM and resources, which can help improve your browsing experience.

Enable hardware acceleration: Hardware acceleration can help improve the performance of your web browser. To enable hardware acceleration in Chromium, open the browser's settings and go to Advanced > Hardware acceleration.

Install extensions: Extensions can add new features and functionality to your web browser. Some popular extensions for Raspberry Pi include AdBlock Plus, Evernote Web Clipper, and Grammarly.

Keep your software up to date: KeePing your web browser and operating system up to date will help ensure that you have the latest security patches and bug fixes.

By following these tips, you can enjoy a fast, secure, and enjoyable browsing experience on your Raspberry Pi 5.

Watching movies and listening to music on the raspberry Pi 5

The Raspberry Pi 5 is a powerful and versatile device that can be used for a variety of tasks, including watching movies and listening to music. There are several different media center applications available for the Raspberry Pi 5, each with its own strengths and weaknesses. Some popular options include Kodi, OSMC, and LibreELEC.

Kodi is a free and open-source media center application that is available for a wide variety of platforms, including the Raspberry Pi 5. It is a powerful and versatile application that can play a wide variety of media files, including videos, music, and podcasts. Kodi also supports a wide variety of add-ons, which can extend its functionality and allow you to customize your experience.

OSMC is a fork of Kodi that is specifically designed for the Raspberry Pi. It is a lightweight and streamlined application that is optimized for use on the Raspberry Pi 5. OSMC is a good option for users who are looking for a simple and easy-to-use media center application.

LibreELEC is another fork of Kodi that is specifically designed for the Raspberry Pi. It is a minimal and lightweight application that is designed for users who want a stripped-down media center experience. LibreELEC is a good option for users who have older Raspberry Pi models or who want a media center application that is easy to install and maintain.

Once you have installed a media center application, you can add your media files to it. You can do this by copying your files to the Raspberry Pi's SD card or by connecting an external hard drive. Once your media files are added, you can start playing them using the media center application's remote control or on-screen interface.

In addition to watching movies and listening to music, you can also use your Raspberry Pi 5 to play games, watch TV shows, and browse the web. With its powerful processor and versatile software, the Raspberry Pi 5 is a great all-around entertainment device.

Here are some tips for watching movies and listening to music with your Raspberry Pi 5:

Use a high-speed HDMI cable: A high-speed HDMI cable will ensure that you get the best Picture quality from your Raspberry Pi 5.

Connect to a high-quality speaker or sound system: A good speaker or sound system will make your movies and music sound even better.

Install a media center add-on for streaming services: There

are many media center add-ons available that allow you to stream movies and music from popular services like Netflix, Spotify, and YouTube.

Use a Raspberry Pi remote control: A Raspberry Pi remote control makes it easy to control your media center application from the comfort of your couch.

By following these tips, you can get the most out of your Raspberry Pi 5 as an entertainment device.

Playing games on the raspberry Pi 5

The Raspberry Pi 5 is a powerful and versatile single-board computer (SBC) that can be used for a wide range of tasks, including gaming. With its improved performance and enhanced capabilities, the Raspberry Pi 5 offers a wider range of gaming options compared to its predecessors.

Emulation: The Raspberry Pi 5's powerful processor and dedicated graphics processor make it an excellent platform for emulating classic consoles. Retro gaming enthusiasts can enjoy a vast library of games from various consoles, including the Nintendo

Entertainment System (NES), Super Nintendo Entertainment System (SNES), Sega Genesis, and Sony PlayStation. Emulators such as RetroPie, Recalbox, and Batocera provide user-friendly interfaces and comprehensive game compatibility.

RetroArch: RetroArch is a versatile emulation platform that supports a wide range of consoles and gaming systems. It offers a unified interface for loading and playing games from various emulators, making it a convenient choice for retro gaming enthusiasts. RetroArch's extensive configuration options allow users to customize their gaming experience.

Native Games: While the Raspberry Pi 5's capabilities are primarily geared towards retro gaming, there are also a number of native games available for the device. These games are tyPically developed using lightweight game engines and frameworks like Pygame and Godot. Some popular native games include:

Minecraft Pi: A special edition of the popular sandbox game Minecraft, optimized for the Raspberry Pi.

Pinball FX2: A Pinball simulation game with various tables and themes.

Quake III Arena: A classic first-person shooter game that has been ported to the Raspberry Pi.

OpenTTD: A free and open-source simulation game insPired by the classic Transport Tycoon.

Sonic Pi: An educational tool that combines coding and music creation, allowing users to create and share their own music.

Online Gaming: The Raspberry Pi 5's connectivity options, including Ethernet and Wi-Fi, make it possible to play online games. However, the device's performance may not be sufficient for demanding online multiplayer titles. Some popular online games that can be played on the Raspberry Pi 5 include:

World of Warships Blitz: A free-to-play action-strategy game featuring naval battles.

Dota 2: A popular multiplayer online battle arena (MOBA) game.

Team Fortress 2: A class-based team-shooting game.

Counter-Strike: Global Offensive: A first-person shooter game with competitive multiplayer modes.

Path of Exile: A free-to-play action role-playing game (ARPG) with dark fantasy elements.

Game Streaming: Game streaming services like Steam Link and Nvidia GeForce Now allow you to stream games from a more powerful computer to your Raspberry Pi 5. This option enables you to play demanding games on your Raspberry Pi without the need for high-end hardware.

Considerations for Gaming on Raspberry Pi:

Performance: The Raspberry Pi 5's performance is suitable for retro gaming and less demanding native games. For more demanding titles, consider using game streaming services or upgrading to a more powerful SBC.

Peripherals: A gamepad or keyboard and mouse are essential for comfortable gaming.

Operating System: Choose an operating system that is optimized for gaming, such as RetroPie or Recalbox for retro gaming or a lightweight Linux distribution for native games.

Game Compatibility: Ensure that the games you want to play are compatible with the chosen emulator or native platform.

Community Support: A large and active community of Raspberry Pi users provides support and resources for gaming on the device.

With its improved capabilities and diverse gaming options, the Raspberry Pi 5 offers a fun and versatile platform for both retro gaming and playing native games. Whether you're a seasoned gamer or a newcomer to the world of Raspberry Pi gaming, there's a wealth of options to explore and enjoy.

CHAPTER THREE

Learning python on the raspberry Pi 5

Learning Python on the Raspberry Pi 5 is an excellent way to get started with programming and explore the capabilities of this versatile single-board computer (SBC). The Raspberry Pi 5's powerful processor and user-friendly environment make it an ideal platform for beginners and experienced programmers alike.

Getting Started with Python on Raspberry Pi 5:

1. Install Python: Python is pre-installed on the Raspberry Pi OS, so you don't need to install it separately. However, ensure you have the latest version installed by updating your system using the terminal command:

```
sudo apt update && sudo apt upgrade
```

2. Choose a Text Editor: A text editor is essential for writing and editing Python code. Popular choices include Thonny, IDLE, and Geany. Thonny is a beginner-friendly editor with a visual debugging interface, while IDLE is the default Python editor on Raspberry Pi OS. Geany is a more advanced text editor with support for various programming languages.

3. Write Your First Python Program: Start with basic Python syntax and concepts, such as variables, data types, operators, and control flow statements. Practice writing simple programs that print messages, perform calculations, and take user input.

4. Explore Python Libraries: Python offers a vast library of modules that extend its functionality. Learn about libraries like NumPy for numerical computing, Matplotlib for data visualization, and Kivy for creating graphical user interfaces.

5. Utilise Raspberry Pi GPiO (General-Purpose Input/Output) Pins: The Raspberry Pi's GPiO Pins allow you to interact with electronics and sensors. Use libraries like RPi.GPiO to control LEDs, read sensor data, and build interactive projects.

6. Engage with the Raspberry Pi Community: The Raspberry

Pi community is a valuable resource for learning and sharing knowledge. Join online forums, attend workshops, and seek help from experienced programmers to enhance your learning experience.

Resources for Learning Python on Raspberry Pi 5:

1. Official Raspberry Pi Python Documentation: Provides comprehensive tutorials and reference guides for Python programming on Raspberry Pi.

2. Learn Python - Free Interactive Python Tutorial: An interactive online tutorial that covers the fundamentals of Python programming.

3. Automate the Boring Stuff with Python: A popular book that teaches Python programming in a practical and engaging way.

4. **Programming for the Raspberry Pi: Getting Started with Python: A beginner-friendly book that guides you through Python programming on the Raspberry Pi.

5. Raspberry Pi Projects with Python: A collection of projects that demonstrate the use of Python on Raspberry Pi, from controlling LEDs to building web servers.

Remember, learning Python is a journey, not a destination. Be patient, consistent, and practice regularly to master the language and create amazing projects with Raspberry Pi.

Creating your first python program on raspberry Pi 5

Creating your first Python program on the Raspberry Pi 5 is an exciting step into the world of programming. Here's a simple guide to get you started:

Step 1: Set Up Your Raspberry Pi 5

1. Install Raspberry Pi OS: Download the Raspberry Pi OS Lite image and install it on a microSD card.

2. Connect Your Raspberry Pi: Connect the microSD card, power supply, HDMI cable, keyboard, and mouse to your Raspberry Pi.

3. Boot Up and Configure: Power on your Raspberry Pi and follow the on-screen instructions to complete the initial setup.

Step 2: Open a Text Editor

1. **Thonny:** Thonny is a beginner-friendly Python IDE that comes pre-installed on Raspberry Pi OS. Click on the Raspberry Pi icon, select "Programming," and then choose "Thonny Python IDE."

2. **Idle:** IDLE is the default Python editor on Raspberry Pi OS. Open the terminal window and type `idle3` to launch the editor.

3. **Geany**: Geany is a more advanced text editor with support for various programming languages. Open the terminal

window and type `sudo apt install geany` to install it. Once installed, type `geany` to launch the editor.

Step 3: Write Your First Program

1. Print a Message: Start by writing a simple program that prints a message to the console. For example:

```python
print("Hello, World!")
```

2. Save the Program: Save your program with a `.py` extension.

For instance, save the above code as `hello_world.py`.

3. Run the Program: In Thonny, click the "Run" button. In IDLE, press F5. In Geany, click on the "Run" button in the toolbar or type `F9`.

Step 4: Experiment with Variables and Data Types

1. Define Variables: Variables store data values. For example:

```python
name = "John Doe"
age = 30
```

2. Data Types: Python has different data types, such as numbers (int, float), strings (str), and booleans (True, False).

Step 5: Explore Control Flow Statements

1. Conditional Statements (if, elif, else): Use these statements to execute different code blocks based on conditions.

2. LooPing Statements (for, while): Use these statements to repeat code blocks multiple times.

Additional Tips:

1. Use Comments:Add comments (lines starting with `#`) to explain your code.

2. Format Your Code: Use proper indentation to make your code easier to read and understand.

3. Seek Help: Utilize online tutorials, documentation, and forums to seek assistance when needed.

Remember, programming is a journey, not a destination. Be patient, practice regularly, and enjoy the process of learning and creating!

Advanced python programming for raspberry Pi 5

Advanced Python programming for Raspberry Pi 5 involves exploring more sophisticated concepts and techniques to develop more complex and powerful applications. Here are some key areas to delve into:

1. Object-Oriented Programming (OOP): OOP is a programming paradigm that emphasizes creating classes and objects to organize and manage code modularity and reusability. Learn about classes, objects, inheritance, polymorphism, and encapsulation to create well-structured and maintainable Python applications.

2. Networking and Communication: Understand how to connect your Raspberry Pi to networks, send and receive data, and interact with other devices. Learn about protocols like TCP/IP, socket programming, and network libraries like requests and scapy to build network-connected applications.

3. Multithreading and Concurrency: Explore ways to handle multiple tasks simultaneously in your Python programs. Learn about multithreading, thread synchronization techniques, and asynchronous programming with libraries like asyncio to improve application responsiveness and performance.

4. Database Programming: Learn how to interact with databases like MySQL, PostgreSQL, or SQLite using Python libraries like SQLAlchemy or psycopg2. Store, retrieve, and manipulate data efficiently to build data-driven applications.

5. Graphical User Interfaces (GUIs): Develop visually appealing and interactive applications using Python GUI frameworks like Tkinter, Kivy, or PyQt. Create user interfaces with widgets, layouts, and event handling to provide a user-friendly experience.

6. Hardware Interfacing: Deepen your understanding of interfacing with hardware components beyond basic GPiO control. Learn about advanced protocols like I2C, SPi, and serial communication to interact with sensors, actuators, and other peripherals.

7. Real-time Programming: Explore real-time programming techniques to handle time-critical applications. Learn about real-time operating systems (RTOS), real-time scheduling algorithms, and real-time programming frameworks like RTCP (Real-Time Control Protocol) and ROS (Robot Operating System).

8. Machine Learning and Artificial Intelligence: Utilize Python's capabilities in machine learning and AI to build intelligent applications. Learn about libraries like TensorFlow, PyTorch, and scikit-learn to train and deploy machine learning models for tasks like classification, regression, and prediction.

9. Web Development: Build web applications and services using Python frameworks like Django, Flask, or Pyramid. Learn about web frameworks, routing, databases, and user authentication to create dynamic and interactive web experiences.

10. Cloud Computing and IoT: Explore cloud platforms like

Amazon Web Services (AWS), Microsoft Azure, or Google Cloud Platform (GCP) to deploy and manage your Python applications on the cloud. Learn about cloud services, APis, and IoT (Internet of Things) protocols to connect your Raspberry Pi to the cloud and build IoT solutions.

Remember, advanced Python programming is a continuous learning process. Engage with the Raspberry Pi community, participate in online forums and workshops, and contribute to open-source projects to expand your knowledge and enhance your skills.

CHAPTER FOUR

Building your raspberry Pi retro gaming console

Building a Raspberry Pi retro gaming console is a fun and rewarding project that allows you to relive your favorite classic video games from the comfort of your own home. With its powerful processor and versatile capabilities, the Raspberry Pi 5 is an ideal platform for emulating a wide range of gaming consoles.

Gather the Necessary Components:

1. Raspberry Pi 5 Board: The Raspberry Pi 5 is the heart of your retro console. It provides the processing power needed to emulate classic gaming systems.

2. MicroSD Card: An 8GB or larger microSD card is recommended to store the operating system, game ROMs, and other files.

3. Power Supply: A 5V/3A power supply unit (PSU) is required to provide sufficient power to the Raspberry Pi 5.

4. HDMI Cable: An HDMI cable is needed to connect the

Raspberry Pi 5 to a monitor or TV for display output.

5. USB Keyboard and Mouse: A USB keyboard and mouse are essential for interacting with the Raspberry Pi 5.

6. Retro Gaming Controller: A gamepad or joystick is recommended for a more authentic retro gaming experience.

Install the Raspberry Pi OS and Emulation Software:

1. Install Raspberry Pi OS Lite: Download and install the

Raspberry Pi OS Lite image onto the microSD card.

2. Configure Raspberry Pi OS: Set up the basic settings of the Raspberry Pi OS, including language, keyboard layout, Wi-Fi connectivity, and user account creation.

3. Install RetroPie: RetroPie is a popular emulation software that provides a user-friendly interface for installing and managing game ROMs. Download and install RetroPie on your Raspberry Pi 5.

4. Add Game ROMs: Download the game ROMs for the consoles you want to emulate. Place the ROMs in the appropriate folders within the RetroPie system.

Connect and Configure Your Retro Gaming Console:

1. Connect the Raspberry Pi 5: Insert the microSD card into the Raspberry Pi 5, connect the power supply, and connect the HDMI cable to your monitor or TV.

2. Connect the Retro Gaming Controller: Plug the USB gamepad or joystick into the Raspberry Pi 5.

3. Configure RetroPie: Launch RetroPie and configure the controls for each gaming system using the controller.

4. Customize RetroPie: Personalize your retro gaming experience by customizing the theme, splash screen, and other settings within RetroPie.

Enjoy Retro Gaming:

1. Select a Console: Choose the console you want to emulate from the RetroPie menu.

2. Browse Game ROMs: Navigate through the game ROM

library and select the game you want to play.

3. Launch the Game: Start the game and enjoy your retro gaming adventure.

Remember that building a Raspberry Pi retro gaming console is an ongoing process. You can continue to add new game ROMs, explore different emulators, and customize your setup to enhance your retro gaming experience.

Creating Home Automation System with the raspberry Pi 5

Creating a home automation system with the Raspberry Pi 5 offers a versatile and customizable approach to controlling and monitoring your home environment. The Raspberry Pi 5's powerful processor and diverse connectivity options make it an ideal platform for automating various tasks and enhancing your living space.

Essential Components for a Home Automation System:

1. Raspberry Pi 5 Board: The Raspberry Pi 5 serves as the central hub for your home automation system, providing the necessary processing power and communication capabilities.

2. Sensors and Actuators: Sensors collect data about the environment, such as temperature, humidity, or motion, while actuators control devices like lights, appliances, or locks.

3. Networking Infrastructure: A reliable Wi-Fi network or Ethernet connection is essential for connecting the Raspberry Pi to sensors, actuators, and the internet.

4. Software and Programming: Home

automation software, such as Home Assistant or OpenHAB, provides the interface for configuring sensors, actuators, and creating rules for automated behavior. Programming knowledge may be required for more complex automation scenarios.

Step-by-Step Guide to Building a Home Automation System:

1. Set Up the Raspberry Pi 5:
Install the Raspberry Pi OS and ensure it is connected to the network.

2. Choose Home Automation Software: Select a suitable home automation software, such as Home Assistant or OpenHAB, and install it on the Raspberry Pi 5.

3. Connect Sensors and Actuators: Connect the sensors and actuators to the Raspberry Pi 5 using appropriate cables or protocols, such as GPiO, I2C, or Zigbee.

4. Configure Sensors and Actuators: Configure the sensors and actuators within the home automation software. Specify measurement ranges, trigger thresholds, and device IDs.

**5. Create Automation Rules:
Define** automation rules that
determine how the actuators
should respond to sensor data.
For instance, turn on lights when
motion is detected or adjust
temperature based on sensor
readings.

6. Test and Refine: Test the
automation rules and make
adjustments as needed.
Continuously monitor and
improve the system's performance
and responsiveness.

**Potential Home Automation
Applications:**

1. Smart Lighting: Control lights based on occupancy, time of day, or ambient light levels.

2. Temperature and Humidity Control: Automate heating and cooling systems to maintain comfortable indoor conditions.

3. Security and Access Control: Implement motion detection alerts, door and window sensors, and smart locks for enhanced security.

4. Energy Management: Monitor and optimize energy

consumption by automating appliance usage and lighting control.

5. Multimedia and Entertainment: Control media playback, streaming services, and home theater systems.

6. Environmental Monitoring: Monitor air quality, water usage, and other environmental factors to promote a healthy home environment.

Remember, building a home automation system is an iterative process. Start with simple automations and gradually expand the system's capabilities as you gain experience and discover new ways to enhance your living space.

Building a weather station with the raspberry Pi 5

Building a weather station with the Raspberry Pi 5 is an exciting project that allows you to collect and monitor real-time weather data from your own backyard. With its powerful capabilities and versatile connectivity options, the Raspberry Pi 5 makes an ideal platform for creating a personalized weather station.

Essential Components for a Weather Station:

1. Raspberry Pi 5 Board: The Raspberry Pi 5 serves as the brain of your weather station, providing the necessary processing power and communication capabilities.

2. Weather Sensors: Sensors collect various meteorological data, such as temperature, humidity, pressure, wind speed, and wind direction.

3. Enclosure: A weatherproof enclosure protects the Raspberry Pi 5 and sensors from the elements.

4.   Networking Infrastructure: A Wi-Fi or Ethernet connection allows the weather station to transmit data to a central server or display.

5.   Software and Programming: Weather station software, such as WeeWX or WeatherDisplay, provides a user-friendly interface for visualizing and analyzing weather data. Programming knowledge may be required for more advanced data processing and visualization.

Step-by-Step Guide to Building a Weather Station:

1. Set Up the Raspberry Pi 5:
Install the Raspberry Pi OS and ensure it is connected to the network.

2. Choose Weather Station Software:
Select a suitable weather station software, such as WeeWX or WeatherDisplay, and install it on the Raspberry Pi 5.

3. Connect Weather Sensors:
Connect the weather sensors to the Raspberry Pi 5 using appropriate cables or protocols, such as GPiO, I2C, or Zigbee.

4. Configure Weather Sensors: Configure the weather sensors within the weather station software. Specify measurement ranges, calibration parameters, and sensor IDs.

5. Install and Configure Data Logger: Install and configure a data logger, such as WeeWX or pyww3, to collect and store weather data from the sensors.

6. Set Up Data Transmission: Configure the data logger to transmit weather data to a central server or display using a suitable communication protocol, such as FTP, MQTT, or webhooks.

7. Create Weather Data Visualization: Design and implement data visualization components within the weather station software or a separate web interface to display real-time and historical weather data.

Potential Weather Station Features:

1. Real-time Weather Monitoring: Display current temperature, humidity, pressure, wind speed, and wind direction.

2. Historical Data Analysis: View trends in weather data over time, such as temperature graphs, humidity charts, and wind direction patterns.

3. Weather Alerts and Notifications: Set up alerts for extreme weather conditions, such as high winds, heavy rain, or sudden temperature drops.

4. Data Sharing and Integration: Share weather data with online weather platforms or integrate it with smart home systems for automated actions.

5. Local Weather Forecast:
Utilize weather data models to generate localized weather forecasts based on current conditions and historical trends.

6. Interactive Weather Dashboard: Create a customizable weather dashboard with interactive widgets, maps, and data visualizations.

Remember, building a weather station is an ongoing process. Continuously monitor and improve the system's accuracy, data transmission reliability, and data visualization effectiveness to enhance your personal weather monitoring experience.

TROUBLESHOOTING RASPBERRY Pi 5 PROBLEMS

Troubleshooting Raspberry Pi 5 problems can range from simple connection issues to more complex software or hardware malfunctions. Here's a step-by-step approach to identify and resolve common problems:

- **1. Check Power Supply:**

- Ensure the power supply is plugged in properly and provides the correct voltage (5V/3A) for the Raspberry Pi 5.

- Try using a different power supply to rule out any issues with the original one.

- 2. **Verify Hardware Connections:**

- Double-check that all cables, including HDMI, power, and any peripherals, are securely connected to their respective ports on the Raspberry Pi 5.

- Try reseating the microSD card to ensure a proper connection.

- **3. Boot Issues:**

- If the Raspberry Pi 5 doesn't boot up properly, check the LED indicators. A solid red LED indicates a hardware issue, while a solid green LED with no video output suggests a problem with the HDMI connection or display.

- Try booting without any peripherals connected to rule out any conflicts.

- **4. Network Connectivity:**

- If you cannot connect to the network, check the Wi-Fi or Ethernet cable connection.

- Restart the router and Raspberry Pi 5 to reset network configurations.

- **5. Software Issues:**

- If the Raspberry Pi 5 is not functioning as expected, try reinstalling the Raspberry Pi OS or updating to the latest version.

- Check for any error messages or warnings in the terminal or log files.

- **6. Overheating:**

- If the Raspberry Pi 5 is overheating, check if the heatsink is properly attached and if there is adequate airflow around the board.

- Consider adding a fan or heatsink enclosure to improve cooling.

- **7. Peripheral Conflicts:**

- If certain peripherals are not working, try connecting them one at a time to identify any conflicts.

- Update drivers or firmware for specific peripherals if available.

- **8. Community Support:**

- Consult online forums, communities, and documentation for specific issues or troubleshooting guides related to the Raspberry Pi 5.

- Engage with experienced users and seek assistance when needed.

GLOSSARY OF RASPBERRY Pi 5 TERMS

Here is a glossary of common Raspberry Pi 5 terms:

ARM Cortex-A76: The CPU architecture used in the Raspberry Pi 5, known for its performance and energy efficiency.

BCM mode: A Pin numbering scheme used for GPiOs on the Raspberry Pi 5.

Bootloader: A small program that starts the Raspberry Pi's operating system when it is powered on.

EEPROM: A type of memory that stores data even when the Raspberry Pi is not powered on.

GPiO (General-Purpose Input/Output): Pins on the Raspberry Pi 5 that can be used to connect to external devices.

HDMI: A type of video interface used to connect the Raspberry Pi 5 to a monitor or TV.

I2C: A type of serial bus used to connect to low-speed devices, such as sensors.

Kernel: The core of the Raspberry Pi's operating system, responsible for managing hardware and software resources.

LED (Light-Emitting Diode): A small electronic component that emits light when it is powered on.

MicroSD card: A type of removable storage that is used to store the Raspberry Pi's operating system and other data.

MIPi CSI-2: A type of camera interface used to connect to high-resolution cameras.

OSMC: A popular media center operating system for the Raspberry Pi.

PWM (Pulse-Width Modulation): A technique used to control the speed of motors or the brightness of LEDs.

RAM (Random Access Memory): The temporary storage used by the Raspberry Pi to store data that is currently being used.

RetroPie: A popular emulation software that allows you to play classic games on the Raspberry Pi.

SD card: A type of removable storage that is used to store the Raspberry Pi's operating system and other data.

SSH (Secure Shell): A protocol that allows you to control the Raspberry Pi remotely from another computer.

UART (Universal Asynchronous Receiver-Transmitter): A type of serial bus used to connect to devices that require serial communication.

USB: A type of bus used to connect to peripherals, such as keyboards, mice, and storage devices.

WiFi: A technology that allows the Raspberry Pi to connect to wireless networks.